CHRISTMAS FACTS UNWRAPPED

Unwrap the Weird, Wonderful and
, Trivia-Filled Side of Christmas

Table of Contents

Introduction

Christmas is a season of joy, traditions, and wonder that brings people together. From decorating trees to singing carols, every custom has a story. This book, with its fun facts, quirky trivia, and festive spirit, is a perfect way to bring your family closer during the holiday season.

Designed for family gatherings or cozy nights by the fire, this book is not just a read, but an experience. It will entertain, educate, and spark laughter. So, grab your cocoa, dive in, and celebrate the magic of Christmas with us!

History and Origins of Christmas

1. **Christmas Celebration Origin:** Christmas dates to the 4th century AD, when the Church officially recognized December 25 as the birthdate of Jesus Christ.

2. **Pre-Christian Roots:** Many Christmas traditions come from pre-Christian winter celebrations, such as Saturnalia in ancient Rome and Yule in Norse mythology.

3. **Pagan Influence:** The ancient Romans celebrated the "Festival of Sol Invictus" (Unconquered Sun) around December 25, likely influencing Christmas customs.

4. **St. Nicholas:** St. Nicholas, the bishop of Myra, inspired Santa Claus. He was known for giving secret gifts to people experiencing poverty.

5. **First Christmas Tree:** The first Christmas tree was recorded in Germany in the 16th century, though it may have earlier roots in pagan traditions.

6. **Christmas and Christ's Birth:** Jesus's exact birth date is unknown, but early Christians adopted December 25 to coincide with existing festivals.

7. **Xmas Abbreviation:** "Xmas" is not a modern invention. The "X" comes from the Greek letter "Chi," the first letter of Χριστός (Christos).

8. Christmas Cards: The first Christmas card was created in 1843 by Sir Henry Cole in England. It featured a family scene and a message of good wishes.

9. Christmas Stockings: The tradition of hanging stockings for Santa to fill is based on the story of St. Nicholas, who secretly put coins in stockings left to dry.

10. Mistletoe: Mistletoe's use during Christmas comes from Norse mythology, where it was seen as a symbol of love and peace.

11. Santa's Reindeer: The names of Santa's reindeer were first introduced in Clement Clarke Moore's 1823 poem "A Visit from St. Nicholas."

12. The Yule Log: The Yule log is a traditional symbol of Christmas. In medieval times, a large log burned throughout the holiday season.

13. The Christmas Feast: The idea of a Christmas feast stems from medieval Europe, where rich meals were prepared to celebrate the season.

14. Advent Calendar: The Advent Calendar has roots in the 19th century. The first was created in Germany, with small doors to open each day until Christmas.

15. Advent Wreath: The Advent wreath, with four candles, was created by Johann Hinrich Wichern in the 19th century to count down the days to Christmas.

16. Epiphany: Epiphany, celebrated on January 6, marks the visit of the Magi to baby Jesus and the end of the Christmas season in many Christian traditions.

17. 12 Days of Christmas: The 12 days begin on December 25 and end on January 5, marking the festive period.

18. Boxing Day: Boxing Day, celebrated in the UK and former British colonies, began as a day to give to people experiencing poverty and to servants after Christmas.

19. First Christmas Tree in America: The first American Christmas tree was planted in 1830 by Pennsylvania German settler.

20. Christmas Tree Decorations: Glass ornaments for Christmas trees became popular in the 19th century after artisans in Germany began producing them.

21. The Nativity Scene: St. Francis of Assisi is credited with creating the first live Nativity scene in 1223, depicting the birth of Jesus.

22. Pope Julius I: Pope Julius I is credited with officially setting December 25 as the date for the celebration of Christmas in the 4th century.

23. Santa Claus Evolution: Coca-Cola popularized the modern image of Santa Claus, with a red suit and white beard, in the 1930s.

24. The Star of Bethlehem: The Star of Bethlehem, which guided the Wise Men to Jesus, is a crucial symbol in the Christmas story.

25. Christmas and the Winter Solstice: Many Christmas customs are tied to the winter solstice, celebrating the sun's rebirth.

26. First Christmas Song: The first known Christmas carol is "Jesus Refulsit Omnium," written in the 4th century.

27. Charles Dickens' Influence: Charles Dickens' novella "A Christmas Carol," published in 1843, had a lasting impact on Christmas traditions and celebrations.

28. Christmas Tree Lighting: The first large-scale public Christmas tree lighting occurred in 1923 in New York City at Rockefeller Centre.

29. Christmas in the Middle Ages: In medieval times, Christmas celebrations were often centred around church services, feasts, and dramatic plays.

30. King's Day: In some countries, such as Spain and Mexico, January 6 is celebrated as King's Day (Día de Reyes) to mark the arrival of the Magi.

Christmas Traditions

31. Christmas Eve: In many cultures, Christmas Eve (December 24) is more important than Christmas Day, with a family meal and gift exchange.

32. Santa Claus: In the U.S., Santa Claus is said to travel around the world on Christmas Eve, aided by his reindeer, delivering presents.

33. Gift Giving: The tradition of exchanging gifts at Christmas comes from the gifts given to the baby Jesus by the Magi.

34. Christmas Lights: The custom of decorating homes with Christmas lights started in the late 19th century when electric lights replaced candles.

35. Candy Canes: Candy canes were invented in the 17th century in Germany and are shaped like shepherd's crooks as a nod to the shepherds in the nativity story.

36. Christmas Dinner: A traditional Christmas meal varies by country but often includes roasted meats, vegetables, and festive desserts.

37. Christmas Pudding: The British Christmas pudding, traditionally made with dried fruits and suet, originated in the 14th century.

38. Ugly Sweater Parties: In the 1980s, the trend of wearing "ugly" Christmas sweaters became popular in the U.S. as a fun holiday tradition.

39. Christmas Carols: Singing Christmas carols dates to the 13th century when they were initially secular songs before becoming associated with the holiday.

40. Nativity Scenes: Displaying a nativity scene is a typical Christmas tradition, especially in Catholic and Christian households.

41. Christmas Stockings: Stockings are traditionally hung by the fireplace for Santa to fill with small gifts and candy.

42. Secret Santa: A fun holiday gift exchange where participants anonymously give presents to one another, often with a budget limit.

43. Christmas Markets: Originating in Germany, Christmas markets are festive events with vendors selling holiday treats, decorations, and gifts.

44. Gingerbread Houses: The tradition of decorating gingerbread houses comes from Germany and was popularized in the U.S. in the 19th century.

45. KFC on Christmas: In Japan, a Christmas meal of fried chicken (often from KFC) has become a popular tradition, starting in the 1970s.

46. Christmas Crackers: A British tradition, Christmas crackers are colourful tubes filled with small toys, jokes, and sometimes paper crowns.

47. Poinsettias: The poinsettia plant, associated with Christmas, is native to Mexico and was introduced to the U.S. in the 19th century.

48. Reindeer Games: The idea of Santa's reindeer playing games stems from the poem "The Night Before Christmas," published in 1823.

49. Christmas Eve Mass: Attending midnight or Christmas Eve services is an essential tradition for many Christian families.

50. Mistletoe Kissing: Kissing under the mistletoe stems from ancient rituals of goodwill and fertility, which evolved into a Christmas custom.

51. Sinterklaas: In the Netherlands and Belgium, children celebrate Sinterklaas (St. Nicholas) before Christmas on December 5 or 6.

52. Twelve Days of Christmas: In some cultures, gifts are exchanged over the twelve days leading up to Epiphany on January 6.

53. Tree Toppers: The star or angel placed atop the Christmas tree symbolizes the Star of Bethlehem or the angel that announced Jesus' birth.

54. Christmas Cribs: Displaying miniature nativity scenes, or "cribs," is widespread, especially in Italy and Spain.

55. New Year's Eve Celebrations: In many countries, New Year's Eve is celebrated with fireworks, parties, and a final festive meal after Christmas.

56. Christmas Sweaters: Christmas-themed sweaters, often with fun or humorous designs, are commonly worn during the holiday season.

57. Christmas Parades: Many cities hold annual parades featuring festive floats, marching bands, and sometimes a Santa Claus appearance.

58. Traditional Christmas Cookies: Baking cookies like sugar cookies, gingerbread men, and shortbread is a beloved holiday activity.

59. Feliz Navidad: The song "Feliz Navidad" was written by José Feliciano in 1970 and is one of the most popular Christmas songs in Spanish-speaking countries.

60. Boxing Day: Boxing Day is celebrated in countries like the UK, Canada, and Australia as a day to give gifts to service workers and charity.

Christmas Movies

61. "Home Alone" (1990): Macaulay Culkin's character, Kevin, has more than 300 tricks up his sleeve to defend his house from burglars.

62. "It's a Wonderful Life" (1946): This classic was initially a box office flop but became one of the most beloved Christmas movies of all time after it entered the public domain in the 1970s.

63. "A Christmas Story" (1983): The film's iconic "Red Ryder BB gun" was inspired by author Jean Shepherd's own childhood Christmas experiences.

64. "The Polar Express" (2004): The movie used groundbreaking motion-capture animation technology to create its distinctive visual style.

65. "Elf" (2003): Will Ferrell, who played Buddy the Elf, ate a plate of spaghetti with syrup for one of the film's most memorable scenes.

66. "Die Hard" (1988): Despite being debated, Die Hard is often considered a Christmas movie due to its Christmas Eve setting and holiday references.

67. "Love Actually" (2003): The movie features multiple intertwined storylines, and its famous "To Me, You Are Perfect" cue card scene was ad-libbed by the actor.

68. "The Grinch Who Stole Christmas" (2000): Jim Carrey's Grinch makeup took about 3 hours to apply each day.

69. "Miracle on 34th Street" (1947): The Macy's department store in the movie is a real store, and they worked closely with the filmmakers to make the film authentic.

70. "National Lampoon's Christmas Vacation" (1989): The Griswold family's Christmas tree was real, and it was so large it could barely fit in the house.

71. "The Nightmare Before Christmas" (1993): Tim Burton came up with the idea for the movie after seeing Halloween decorations that looked like they belonged in a Christmas world.

72. "A Charlie Brown Christmas" (1965): The famous "Christmas Tree" in the movie was a real tree, and it was chosen for its scraggly appearance.

73. "The Santa Clause" (1994): Tim Allen's character, Scott Calvin, transforms into Santa Claus after the original Santa falls off his roof, and the contract he reads was written specifically for the film.

74. "Frosty the Snowman" (1969): Frosty's voice was provided by actor Jackie Vernon, and the song was adapted from the famous Christmas song.

75. "Bad Santa" (2003): Billy Bob Thornton's portrayal of the title character is known for its irreverent, dark humour, setting it apart from traditional Christmas movies.

76. "The Muppets Christmas Carol" (1992): This version of A Christmas Carol is one of the few films where Jim Henson's Muppets bring a classic story to life.

77. "Home Alone 2: Lost in New York" (1992): The Plaza Hotel scene was filmed in New York City, and the hotel itself allowed the filmmakers to shoot on location.

78. "Jingle All the Way" (1996): Arnold Schwarzenegger starred in this holiday comedy about a dad desperately searching for a toy for his son on Christmas Eve.

79. "Scrooged" (1988): This modern retelling of A Christmas Carol stars Bill Murray as a cynical television executive who learns the true meaning of Christmas.

80. "Gremlins" (1984): The movie is set during Christmas, but it's a horror-comedy that blends holiday cheer with terror.

81. "Arthur Christmas" (2011): This animated film explains how Santa delivers presents to every child in one night, using an army of high-tech helpers.

82. "Holiday Inn" (1942): Bing Crosby's song "White Christmas" was first introduced in this musical, making it one of the most famous holiday songs in history.

83. "The Christmas Chronicles" (2018): Kurt Russell plays Santa Claus, and the movie features a nontraditional, action-packed take on the holiday.

84. "Elf" (2003): The North Pole scenes were filmed in an abandoned train station in Vancouver, Canada.

85. "Home Alone" (1990): The house featured in the movie is located in Winnetka, Illinois, and has become a popular tourist attraction during the holidays.

86. "A Christmas Carol" (1951): Alastair Sim's portrayal of Ebenezer Scrooge in this British version of the story is often considered the best cinematic interpretation.

87. "The Holiday" (2006): Kate Winslet and Cameron Diaz play women who swap homes for the holiday season in this romantic comedy.

88. "Rudolph the Red-Nosed Reindeer" (1964): The stop-motion animated special was the longest-running prime-time TV special, airing every year since its debut.

89. "The Family Stone" (2005): This film explores family dynamics over the Christmas holiday and features an ensemble cast including Diane Keaton and Sarah Jessica Parker.

90. "Krampus" (2015): This dark holiday comedy-horror film is based on the legend of Krampus, the Christmas demon who punishes naughty children

Christmas Songs

91. "Jingle Bells": Originally written for Thanksgiving, "Jingle Bells" became one of the most popular Christmas songs ever.

92. "White Christmas": Bing Crosby's version of "White Christmas" remains the best-selling single ever.

93. "Silent Night": This Christmas carol was first performed in 1818 in Austria, and its original lyrics were written in German.

94. "All I Want for Christmas Is You": Mariah Carey's hit has been a holiday staple since its release in 1994 and consistently tops holiday charts.

95. "Last Christmas": Written by George Michael and released by Wham! in 1984, this song is still one of the most-played holiday tracks in the world.

96. "Do They Know It's Christmas?": Released in 1984 by Band-Aid, it raised millions of dollars for famine relief in Ethiopia.

97. "Frosty the Snowman": Based on the popular song of the same name, this was adapted into an animated television special in 1969.

98. "Happy Xmas (War Is Over)": John Lennon and Yoko Ono released this Christmas song in 1971 with a powerful anti-war message to promote peace.

99. "Rudolph the Red-Nosed Reindeer": Written by Johnny Marks and first recorded in 1949 by Gene Autry, it became one of the best-selling holiday songs ever.

100. "The Christmas Song (Chestnuts Roasting on an Open Fire)": Nat King Cole's version of this holiday classic is one of the most recognizable renditions.

101. "Hark! The Herald Angels Sing": Written by Charles Wesley and first published in 1739, this melody is considered one of the most beloved Christmas songs.

102. "Jingle Bell Rock": Released in 1957 by Bobby Helms, it quickly became a Christmas favourite.

103. "I Saw Mommy Kissing Santa Claus": First recorded by Jimmy Boyd in 1952, it sparked some controversy for its playful and innocent take on the Christmas holiday.

104. "Little Drummer Boy": This song, written by Katherine K. Davis, was first recorded in 1958 by the Trapp Family Singers and has since become a holiday standard.

105. "O Holy Night": The song was composed by Adolphe Adam in 1847 and became an instant Christmas classic, celebrated for its powerful lyrics.

106. "Blue Christmas": Originally recorded by Doye O'Dell in 1948, Elvis Presley's 1957 version of "Blue Christmas" became the most famous.

107. "Carol of the Bells": A Ukrainian folk song composed by Mykola Leontovych in 1914 and has since been adapted into many different versions.

108. "Wonderful Christmastime": Paul McCartney released this holiday hit in 1979, and it remains one of his most famous solo tracks.

109. "Silver Bells": Written by Jay Livingston and Ray Evans in 1950, it became a popular Christmas song and was first recorded by Bing Crosby and Carol Richards.

110. "Grandma Got Run Over by a Reindeer": Released in 1979 by Elmo and Patsy, this humorous holiday song has become a Christmas novelty classic.

111. "O Come, All Ye Faithful": The traditional Christmas carol was originally written in Latin in the 18th century.

112. "Here Comes Santa Claus": Written by Gene Autry in 1947, his experiences inspired it with Santa Claus parades in Los Angeles.

113. "Do You Hear What I Hear?": Written in 1962 by Noël Regney and Gloria Shayne, it was inspired by the Cuban Missile Crisis and the desire for peace.

114. "The First Noel": This carol originates in 18th-century England and has been sung by choirs worldwide during Christmas.

115. "Away in a Manger": This melody is one of the most beloved Christmas hymns, often sung in churches worldwide.

116. "Thank God It's Christmas": A song by Queen, released in 1984, that became a Christmas favourite despite not being a major chart hit.

117. "We Wish You a Merry Christmas": A traditional English carol that dates to the 16th century, it is often sung during the holiday season to spread cheer.

118. "Santa Baby": First performed by Eartha Kitt in 1953, the song became a holiday classic known for its playful and cheeky lyrics.

119. "I'll Be Home for Christmas": Written during World War II, this song captured soldiers' longing to be home for the holidays.

120. "Deck the Halls": This melody originates from Wales, has been sung in various versions for centuries, and is one of the most recognizable holiday songs.

Christmas Food and Drink

121. Eggnog: A classic Christmas drink made from milk, sugar, and eggs, and often spiced with nutmeg or cinnamon, with or without alcohol.

122. Minced Pies: Traditionally eaten in the UK, these small pies are filled with spiced fruit and are often associated with Christmas.

123. Fruitcake: The Christmas fruitcake, made with candied fruits, nuts, and spices, has been a holiday staple since the Middle Ages.

124. Christmas Ham: Roasting ham for Christmas dinner is a tradition in many countries, often glazed with honey, brown sugar, or mustard.

125. Sugar Cookies: Baking and decorating sugar cookies is a popular Christmas tradition, especially in North America.

126. Roast Turkey: In many countries, especially the United States, roast turkey is the centrepiece of the Christmas meal.

127. Candy Canes: These sweet, striped candies shaped like a shepherd's crook are a favourite holiday treat.

128. Christmas Pudding: A traditional British dessert, often served with brandy butter or custard, made from dried fruits and suet.

129. Gingerbread Cookies: Popular during Christmas, these spiced cookies are often cut into fun shapes like gingerbread men or houses.

130. Hot Chocolate: A warm, comforting drink many enjoy during Christmas, often topped with marshmallows or whipped cream.

131. Cranberry Sauce: This tangy, sweet sauce is a typical side dish during Christmas meals, particularly with turkey.

132. Roast Vegetables: Along with meats, roast vegetables like potatoes, carrots, and parsnips accompany the Christmas feast.

133. Plum Pudding: Another variation of Christmas pudding, rich with dried fruits and often served with brandy butter.

134. Tarts: Various sweet tarts, such as lemon or cranberry, are popular festive treats in many cultures.

135. Mince Meat: This refers to a spiced filling made from dried fruit, suet, and spices, used in pies or as a condiment in Christmas dishes.

136. Yule Log Cake: A sponge cake shaped like a log, often decorated with icing and powdered sugar to resemble bark, is a favourite Christmas dessert in France.

137. Chestnuts: Roasting chestnuts during the holiday season is often enjoyed by street vendors in many cities.

138. Mulled Wine: A warm, spiced wine typically served during the colder months, especially during Christmas parties or gatherings.

139. Christmas Casseroles: Casseroles such as macaroni and cheese or green bean casserole are often served alongside Christmas meals in the U.S.

140. Fruit Salad: A fresh salad made with winter fruits, such as oranges, apples, and pomegranates, is a popular side dish.

141. Christmas Crackers: Although a tradition in the UK, Christmas crackers—filled with small gifts, jokes, and paper crowns—are often placed at the dinner table.

142. Tiramisu: This Italian dessert, made with layers of coffee-soaked ladyfingers and mascarpone cheese, is a festive favourite for many.

143. Panettone: A sweet, yeasty bread filled with dried fruits, panettone is traditionally enjoyed in Italy and other countries during Christmas.

144. Christmas Ale: Many breweries release unique "Christmas beers" during the holiday season, often spiced with cinnamon, ginger, or other flavours.

145. Sausage Rolls: A British favourite, these pastry-wrapped sausages are often served as appetizers or snacks at Christmas parties.

146. Stuffing: A savory side dish often made with bread, herbs, and vegetables, commonly served with turkey or ham during Christmas dinner.

147. Pecan Pie: A rich, sweet pie made with pecans and syrup; pecan pie is a classic dessert in the Southern United States.

148. Brandy Butter: This rich spread is traditionally served with Christmas pudding in the UK, made from butter, sugar, and brandy.

149. Eggnog Lattes: A seasonal variant of the popular coffee drink, eggnog lattes are a favourite at coffee shops around the holidays.

150. Bûche de Noël: A traditional French Christmas dessert shaped like a log, made with sponge cake, chocolate buttercream, and festive decorations.

Christmas Around the World

151. Australia: Christmas in Australia falls during the summer, so many Australians celebrate with beach barbecues and outdoor activities.

152. Mexico: In Mexico, "Las Posadas" is celebrated from December 16 to 24, reenacting Mary and Joseph's search for shelter.

153. Italy: In Italy, Christmas is celebrated with a huge family feast on Christmas Eve, followed by Mass at church and a festive lunch on Christmas Day.

154. Germany: Christmas markets, known as "Weihnachtsmärkte," are an essential part of Christmas celebrations in Germany.

155. Sweden: In Sweden, Christmas begins with the "Lussekatter" festival on December 13, where saffron buns are eaten.

156. Japan: In Japan, Christmas is not a national holiday, but many celebrate with fried chicken meals, and some exchange Christmas cakes.

157. Finland: Christmas Eve is the main holiday in Finland, and families often visit cemeteries to honour deceased loved ones.

158. France: In France, the "Réveillon" is a festive meal on Christmas Eve, followed by the exchange of gifts at midnight.

159. Philippines: Christmas celebrations in the Philippines are among the longest in the world, starting as early as September.

160. Norway: In Norway, Christmas Eve is celebrated with a festive meal and the lighting of candles. Norwegians also enjoy a game of "julebukk" (Christmas goat).

161. Russia: Russian Orthodox Christians celebrate Christmas on January 7, according to the Julian calendar.

162. Greece: In Greece, Christmas Eve is marked by singing carols, and the Christmas Day meal often includes lamb or pork.

163. Poland: In Poland, Christmas Eve dinner consists of twelve dishes, one for each apostle, and the meal begins after the first star appears in the sky.

164. Denmark: A traditional Christmas dinner in Denmark includes roast duck or pork, followed by rice pudding with a hidden almond.

165. Iceland: Iceland celebrates Christmas with the "Yule Lads," 13 mischievous figures who visit children during the 13 days leading up to Christmas.

166. Ireland: In Ireland, Christmas Eve is often celebrated with a family gathering, and Christmas Day begins with Mass, followed by a large family meal.

167. United Kingdom: In the UK, the Christmas meal traditionally features roast turkey, Christmas pudding, and crackers with small gifts.

168. Czech Republic: In the Czech Republic, Christmas Eve dinner is meatless, often featuring fish soup, carp, and potato salad.

169. South Africa: Christmas falls during summer in South Africa, so many celebrate with outdoor barbecues or picnics.

170. Canada: Christmas is a significant holiday in Canada, with Christmas Eve often marked by midnight Mass and Christmas Day spent with family.

171. Brazil: Christmas in Brazil is celebrated with a festive meal that includes roasted meats, rice, and tropical fruits, along with fireworks at midnight.

172. India: In India, Christmas is celebrated with church services, festive meals, and the decoration of homes with stars and lights.

173. Belgium: In Belgium, Saint Nicholas' Day (December 6) is a major holiday, with the Christmas season officially beginning after this date.

174. Hungary: Christmas in Hungary is celebrated with a large meal, often featuring fish soup, stuffed cabbage, and a Christmas tree adorned with homemade decorations.

175. Latvia: In Latvia, Christmas Eve is the most essential part of the holiday, marked by a family meal and a visit from Jõuluvana (Father Christmas).

176. Ukraine: Ukrainians celebrate Christmas with a 12-course dinner on Christmas Eve, each dish representing an apostle, followed by church services.

177. Ethiopia: In Ethiopia, Christmas is celebrated on January 7, known as "Genna," where people fast until after the church service.

178. South Korea: In South Korea, Christmas is a public holiday, but it is primarily celebrated by Christians, with church services and family gatherings.

179. Turkey: Christmas is celebrated in Turkey with church services, festive meals, and the decoration of homes, but it is not as widely observed as in Western countries.

180. New Zealand: Like Australia, Christmas in New Zealand is celebrated during the summer with barbecues, outdoor activities, and beach outings.

Christmas Symbols and Decorations

181. Christmas Tree: The Christmas tree originated in 16th-century Germany, decorated with candles and edible treats.

182. Star of Bethlehem: The Star of Bethlehem symbolizes the guiding light that led the Magi to the birthplace of Jesus.

183. Christmas Angel: Angels are often used in Christmas decorations to symbolize the announcement of Jesus' birth to the shepherds.

184. Candy Cane: The candy cane's shape resembles a shepherd's crook, symbolizing Jesus as the "Good Shepherd."

185. Wreath: The circular wreath represents eternity and is often used to decorate doors during Christmas.

186. Poinsettias: These red and green flowers, native to Mexico, are a popular Christmas decoration because they symbolize Christ's blood.

187. Mistletoe: Mistletoe is hung as a tradition for couples to kiss under it, symbolizing love and peace.

188. Tinsel: Tinsel, originally made from silver, is draped over Christmas trees to add sparkle and represent the light of Christ.

189. Santa Claus: Santa Claus is based on St. Nicholas, a 4th-century Christian bishop known for his generosity to children.

190. Reindeer: Reindeer are closely associated with Christmas, particularly the legend of Santa's sleigh, which eight reindeer pull.

191. Christmas Lights: The tradition of decorating with lights started in the 17th century and has become a crucial part of holiday celebrations.

192. Stockings: The tradition of hanging stockings comes from the story of St. Nicholas, who dropped gold coins into socks left by children.

193. Gingerbread Houses: Gingerbread houses became a tradition in the 16th century and are often decorated with candy during the holiday season.

194. Christmas Cards: The tradition of sending Christmas cards began in England in the 1840s, with the first commercial Christmas card being created by artist John Calcott Horsley.

195. Bells: Bells are used as a Christmas decoration and symbol, signifying joy and the arrival of Christ.

196. Nativity Scene: The nativity scene, depicting the birth of Jesus, was first created by St. Francis of Assisi in the 13th century.

197. Yule Log: The Yule log was originally an ancient European tradition that involved burning a large log in the hearth during Christmas.

198. Snowflakes: Snowflakes are often used in decorations to represent the purity and beauty of the season.

199. Christmas Eve Candle: Lighting a candle on Christmas Eve symbolizes the arrival of Christ as the Light of the World.

200. Holly: Holly is often used in Christmas decorations and symbolizes eternal life, with its red berries representing the blood of Christ.

201. Crackers: Christmas crackers, a UK tradition, are pulled apart by two people to reveal small gifts, jokes, and a paper crown.

202. Santa's Sleigh: Santa's sleigh, drawn by reindeer, is a central part of the Christmas mythos, symbolizing the magical nature of the holiday.

203. Christmas Cookies: Decorating cookies, especially gingerbread men and sugar cookies, are famous in many homes.

204. Icicles: Icicle decorations, often placed on trees or houses, mimic the natural beauty of winter and symbolize purity and elegance.

205. Christmas Tree Ornaments: Ornaments, such as glass baubles, angels, and stars, decorate Christmas trees, symbolizing joy and celebration.

206. Snowmen: Snowmen are made from snow during winter and often become part of Christmas yard displays.

207. Carolling Books: Carolling books contain lyrics to popular Christmas songs and are often used during Christmas carol singing.

208. Frosty Windowpanes: In some parts of the world, frost on windows is a common sight during Christmas, adding to the holiday atmosphere.

209. Christmas Table Settings: Special Christmas-themed tableware and utensils are used for festive meals, often adorned with red, green, or gold.

210. Snow Globes: Snow globes are decorative ornaments filled with water and glitter, often depicting Christmas scenes that resemble winter wonderlands.

Christmas Traditions and Customs

211. Advent Calendar: The Advent calendar tradition originated in Germany in the 19th century and is used to count down the days until Christmas.

212. Secret Santa: The custom of Secret Santa, where people exchange anonymous gifts, is widely practiced during Christmas.

213. Christmas Carols: Singing carols door-to-door, known as "carolling," is a tradition where groups sing festive songs to spread holiday cheer.

214. Yule Log: The Yule log tradition involves burning a large log in the fireplace on Christmas Eve for luck, symbolizing the sun's return.

215. Boxing Day: Celebrated on December 26th, Boxing Day originated in the UK and is known for charitable giving and post-Christmas sales.

216. Christmas Markets: Christmas markets, particularly in Europe, are an iconic tradition where people shop for festive foods, gifts, and decorations.

217. The Christmas Pickle: An unusual tradition where a glass pickle ornament is hidden on the Christmas tree, and the first person to find it gets an extra gift.

218. Kris Kringle: In many countries, particularly in the U.S. and Germany, "Kris Kringle" is another name for Santa Claus, derived from the German "Christ kind."

219. Twelve Days of Christmas: The Twelve Days of Christmas, from December 25th to January 5th, commemorate the period between Christ's birth and Epiphany.

220. Christmas Eve Dinner: In many European countries, Christmas Eve dinner is a big family gathering with traditions such as fasting until the meal or enjoying a feast of twelve dishes.

221. Elf on the Shelf: The Elf on the Shelf is a modern tradition where a tiny elf moves around the house each night, "watching" children's behaviour until Christmas.

222. Christmas Pyjamas: A relatively modern custom is for families to receive or buy matching pyjamas worn on Christmas Eve for a cozy holiday spirit.

223. Poinsettia Giving: Giving poinsettias as gifts is a tradition in Mexico, where they are often associated with Christmas and symbolize the Star of Bethlehem.

224. Holiday Baking: Many families have the tradition of baking cookies, cakes, or bread to enjoy or give as gifts to loved ones during the holiday season.

225. Mummering: In Newfoundland and parts of the U.S. and Canada, "mummering" involves people dressing in disguise and visiting neighbours for festive fun during Christmas.

226. Christmas Eve Service: Many Christians attend a midnight mass or church service on Christmas Eve, often to celebrate the birth of Jesus Christ.

227. Saint Nicholas Day: Celebrated on December 6th, this holiday honours St. Nicholas and is widely observed in countries like the Netherlands and Germany.

228. Tree Lighting Ceremonies: In many cities, the lighting of the Christmas tree is a significant event, often featuring music, entertainment, and a large crowd.

229. Hanukkah and Christmas Together: In some Jewish families, Hanukkah and Christmas overlap, with traditions from both holidays being celebrated.

230. Christmas Shoes: The "Christmas Shoes" tradition, based on a song and story, reflects the spirit of giving to those in need during the holiday season.

231. Luminarias: In Southwestern U.S. states, particularly New Mexico, Christmas Eve is celebrated with luminarias—small paper lanterns or candles placed along pathways.

232. Wassailing: Wassailing, a centuries-old tradition in the UK, involves singing carols to the trees to ensure a good apple harvest for the following year.

233. Scrooge and Marley: The "Scrooge and Marley" tradition, inspired by Charles Dickens's A Christmas Carol, involves reenacting or reading the famous Christmas tale.

234. Gift Wrapping Parties: In some places, families and friends gather before Christmas to wrap gifts together while enjoying snacks and drinks.

235. Christmas Eve Gifts: In some countries, like Denmark and Norway, families exchange gifts on Christmas Eve rather than Christmas morning.

236. Hogmanay: In Scotland, New Year's Eve, known as Hogmanay, is often as important as Christmas itself, with unique customs like "first-footing."

237. Gingerbread House Decorating: Decorating gingerbread houses is a fun family tradition trendy in Scandinavia and North America.

238. Christmas Day Parade: Cities like New York host large parades on Christmas Day, often featuring floats, bands, and holiday performances.

239. Sinterklaas: In the Netherlands, Sinterklaas arrives on December 5th, a celebration marked by parades, gifts, and sweets, like Santa Claus.

240. The ringing of the Bells: Churches worldwide ring bells on Christmas Eve or Christmas Day to announce the birth of Christ.

Christmas Myths and Legends

241. The Origins of Santa Claus: Santa Claus is based on the real-life Saint Nicholas, a 4th-century Christian bishop known for his generosity toward children.

242. Reindeer Names: Santa's reindeer—Dasher, Dancer, Prancer, Vixen, Comet, Cupid, Donder, and Blitzen—were popularized by the 1823 poem A Visit from St. Nicholas.

243. The Grinch: Dr. Seuss' character, the Grinch, is a beloved holiday villain who eventually learns the true meaning of Christmas in his iconic tale.

244. Rudolph the Red-Nosed Reindeer: the famous reindeer with a glowing red nose was created in 1939 by Robert L. May for a Montgomery Ward Christmas booklet.

245. The Nutcracker: The Nutcracker ballet, based on a story by E.T.A. Hoffmann, features a magical adventure and has become a Christmas tradition since its 1892 premiere.

246. Krampus: Krampus, a half-goat, half-demon figure from Central European folklore, punishes misbehaving children during the Christmas season.

247. Father Christmas vs. Santa Claus: Father Christmas is the British counterpart to Santa Claus, and while they share many similarities, Father Christmas is more focused on the spirit of Christmas.

248. The Christmas Ghosts: According to the legend in A Christmas Carol, Scrooge is visited by three ghosts (Past, Present, and Yet to Come) on Christmas Eve to teach him the importance of generosity.

249. The Christmas Spider: A Ukrainian legend claims that a spider decorated a Christmas tree with webs, which turned into silver and gold, making spiders a symbol of good luck.

250. Twelve Days of Christmas: The "Twelve Days of Christmas" is a song and a reference to the period between Christmas and Epiphany, with each day representing a different gift.

251. Pinecones and Christmas: Pinecones symbolize eternal life and are often used in Christmas decorations due to their association with the Christmas tree.

252. The Christmas Star: The Star of Bethlehem is said to have guided the three wise men to the birthplace of Jesus.

253. Mistletoe's Magic: In Norse mythology, mistletoe symbolizes love and is believed to have the power to bring peace and happiness.

254. The Legend of the Christmas Carol: Charles Dickens's A Christmas Carol was inspired by his desire to raise awareness of people experiencing poverty and to challenge Victorian social values.

255. Santa's Workshop: The idea of Santa's magical workshop at the North Pole, where elves make toys, became popular in the 19th century, bolstered by poems and stories.

256. The Christmas Angel: Angels are believed to have appeared to the shepherds to announce the birth of Jesus, making them a central symbol of Christmas.

257. Christmas Eve Miracle: In some cultures, it is believed that miracles can happen on Christmas Eve, including spontaneous healings or sudden changes in fortune.

258. St. Lucia's Day: In Sweden, the story of St. Lucia, the patron saint of light, is celebrated with processions of girls dressed in white robes and wearing candles on their heads.

259. The Legend of Santa's Reindeer: In addition to the famous reindeer names, some legends add additional reindeer, such as the "ninth" reindeer named "Olive," as in the joke, "Olive, the other reindeer."

260. Gifts from the Wise Men: The gifts that the three wise men brought to Jesus—gold, frankincense, and myrrh—have symbolic meanings tied to Jesus' identity as king, deity, and sacrifice.

261. St. Nicholas and the Shoes: The tradition of placing shoes out for St. Nicholas to fill with gifts is said to have originated with the saint's acts of charity.

262. The Yule Goat: The Yule Goat is a Scandinavian Christmas figure thought to be a bringer of gifts, and its origins date back to pre-Christian winter festivals.

263. The Christmas Witch (La Befana): In Italy, La Befana is a kindly old witch who delivers gifts to children on Epiphany Eve, often sweeping the floors before she leaves.

264. The Legend of the Christmas Rose: In European folklore, the Christmas Rose is said to bloom around Christmas and symbolizes hope and renewal.

265. Santa's Elves: The image of Santa's elves, tiny, magical workers who make toys, evolved from folk tales and literature in the 19th century.

266. The Christmas Tree Angel: The tradition of placing an angel atop the Christmas tree symbolizes the angels who announced the birth of Jesus to the shepherds.

267. Frosty the Snowman: a jolly snowman brought to life by a magical hat became a holiday favourite after the song Frosty the Snowman was released in 1950.

268. Christmas Eve Traditions in Mexico: In Mexico, Nochebuena (Christmas Eve) is celebrated with a large family feast, fireworks, and the reenactment of the Nativity story.

269. The Christmas Bell: Some believe that the ringing of a Christmas bell signifies that an angel has earned their wings.

270. St. Nicholas' Miracles: The real-life St. Nicholas was credited with many miracles, including saving sailors and providing dowries for poor girls, contributing to his image as a gift-bringer.

Christmas Science Facts

271. Snowflakes' Unique Structures: Every snowflake is unique due to the way water molecules arrange themselves as they freeze. The shape is influenced by temperature and humidity during its fall.

272. Why Snow is White: Snow looks white because its ice crystals reflect and scatter light in all directions, which gives it a bright, white appearance.

273. The Physics of Snowflakes: Snowflakes are made of tiny ice crystals forming in clouds when water vapor freezes. The molecular structure of ice gives them their six-pointed shape.

274. The Speed of Santa's Sleigh: To visit all the homes in one night, Santa would need to travel at over 6,000 miles per second, much faster than the speed of sound!

275. The Christmas Tree's Carbon Impact: A real Christmas tree absorbs carbon dioxide from the air while it grows, helping reduce greenhouse gases.

276. Electric Christmas Lights: Today's Christmas lights use LED technology, which consumes less electricity and lasts longer than traditional incandescent bulbs.

277. The Science of Christmas Tree Ornaments: Many Christmas ornaments, especially glass ones, are made by blowing glass, which involves molten glass being inflated into hollow shapes.

278. The Chemistry of Candy Canes: The red and white stripes on a candy cane are formed from sugar syrup that's boiled to a specific temperature and then stretched until it cools.

279. The Temperature of Ice Cream for Santa: Ice cream in a freezer is typically stored at about -20°F (-29°C), but it becomes harder and colder the longer it stays in the freezer.

280. Why Mistletoe Is Poisonous: Mistletoe contains toxins, like Visco toxin, that can harm humans if ingested. This is why it's best used for decoration, not for consumption.

281. How Reindeer Can Survive the Cold: Reindeer (caribou) have specialized fur that insulates them from the cold. Their hooves are also uniquely adapted to help them walk on snow and ice.

282. The Physics of Santa's Sleigh: If Santa's sleigh is to defy physics and fly around the world, we'd need to account for wind resistance, gravity, and air pressure – but Christmas magic would need to be involved!

283. How Christmas Lights Work: Traditional Christmas lights use incandescent bulbs, which heat a filament to produce light. Modern LED lights emit light more efficiently using semiconductors.

284. Why Christmas Lights Flicker: Flickering Christmas lights can occur when the circuit is faulty, a bulb is slightly loose, or the current flowing through the lights is not steady.

285. The Role of Polar Bears in Climate Change: Polar bears, iconic symbols of the winter season, are increasingly threatened by climate change due to the melting of the Arctic ice where they live.

286. The Chemical Reaction of Christmas Pudding: Traditional Christmas puddings rely on a complex chemical process, where ingredients like suet and treacle interact under heat to produce a rich, sticky texture.

287. How Snowflakes Form: Snowflakes form when water vapor freezes around dust particles in the atmosphere. The temperature and humidity determine the snowflake's shape at the formation time.

288. The Physics of Sleigh Bells: The ringing of sleigh bells results from vibration caused by the movement of the sleigh and the small metal balls inside the bell striking the sides.

289. Why Christmas Trees Smell So Good: Christmas trees release oils and chemicals like pinene, which gives them their signature pine scent. This is due to the tree's natural defense mechanisms.

290. The Science of Hot Chocolate: The perfect hot chocolate involves dissolving cocoa powder and sugar in milk or water. Milk helps distribute cocoa's fat molecules, giving the drink its creamy texture.

291. How Christmas Stockings Stay Hung: The physics of stockings involves the balance of weight distribution. If the stocking is too heavy, the hook or mantle must counterbalance the weight to prevent it from falling.

292. Why We Get Cold Noses at Christmas: During the winter, the body's blood vessels constrict to preserve heat, making the nose more prone to feeling cold. The face is also often the first to lose warmth.

293. How the Nutcracker Works: The Nutcracker uses mechanical leverage to crack open nuts, with a simple class of physics: pressure applied by the handle is concentrated on the nut, causing it to crack.

294. How Ice Melts on Roads: Salting roads during the winter lowers the freezing point of water, causing ice to melt even when the temperature is below the usual freezing point of water ($32°F/0°C$).

295. Why Hot Water Freezes Faster Than Cold: This is called the Mpemba effect, where, under certain conditions, hot water freezes faster than cold due to changes in the properties of water molecules.

296. The Chemistry of the Christmas Ham: When you cook a ham, the heat causes proteins in the meat to break down, changing the structure and giving the ham its tender texture and delicious taste.

297. How Christmas Lights Stay Safe: Christmas lights often have a built-in fuse to prevent overheating. If too much electricity flows through the circuit, the fuse blows, preventing fire hazards.

298. The Science of Christmas Snow: Snow forms from water vapor that cools and freezes in the atmosphere. The intricate patterns of snowflakes occur due to water molecules forming specific types of bonds.

299. Reindeer's Nose and Global Warming: Reindeer noses help warm the cold air they breathe in, a biological adaptation that prevents their lungs from freezing. This adaptation is significant as Arctic temperatures rise due to global warming.

300. How Artificial Snow Is Made: Artificial snow is created using machines that spray a fine mist of water into cold air. As the mist hits the ground, it freezes instantly, forming snowflakes in a controlled environment.

Christmas Travel

301. Increased Travel During the Holidays: Christmas is one of the busiest times for travel, with millions of people flying, driving, or taking trains to visit family or go on vacation.

302. The Most Travelled Day: The days leading up to Christmas (especially December 23) and the day after Christmas (December 26) are the year's busiest travel days.

303. Christmas Travel and Weather: In many parts of the world, the winter weather plays a significant role in holiday travel. Snowstorms, freezing rain, and icy roads often cause travel delays during the season.

304. Christmas in the Caribbean: Many people travel to warmer climates during the holidays. The Caribbean is a popular destination for Christmas getaways, offering tropical warmth and festive celebrations.

305. Largest Christmas Parade: The largest Christmas parade occurs in Kissimmee, Florida. It includes floats, marching bands, and a variety of performers.

306. Holiday Train Travel: In places like Switzerland and Canada, scenic holiday train rides (like the Polar Express) are a popular way to travel and experience winter landscapes during Christmas.

307. Airports Are Packed: The Christmas season leads to significant airport congestion. Airports like Hartsfield-Jackson Atlanta International are among the busiest in the world during this time.

308. The Christmas Markets in Europe: Christmas markets in cities like Munich, Vienna, and Nuremberg attract millions of tourists yearly for holiday shopping, festive foods, and mulled wine.

309. Traveling for Christmas Eve Services: Many people travel to attend Christmas Eve church services, especially in countries with strong Christian traditions, such as Italy, Poland, and Mexico.

310. Travel for Christmas Shopping: Christmas shopping trips can involve extensive travel, especially to major retail hubs like New York City, London, and Paris, where holiday lights and displays draw in shoppers from around the world.

311. Christmas in New York City: New York City is a holiday travel hotspot. People from all over the world visit to see the famous Rockefeller Christmas Tree, Ice Skating Rinks, and shops along Fifth Avenue.

312. Overseas Travel for Christmas: In the UK, many people travel abroad to celebrate Christmas in warmer climates, especially to destinations like Spain, Portugal, and the Canary Islands.

313. Christmas Cruises: Many families take Christmas-themed cruises to destinations like the Caribbean, Alaska, or Hawaii. The festive atmosphere aboard the ships often includes special holiday activities.

314. Ski Resorts and Christmas Travel: Ski resorts in destinations like the Swiss Alps, Aspen, and Whistler become major Christmas travel spots, with visitors flocking for winter sports and cozy mountain cabins.

315. Festive Train Journeys: The "Polar Express" train ride is a holiday Favorite for families in the United States, especially in places like Williams, Arizona, and North Carolina.

316. Traveling for Christmas Lights: In the United States, places like McAdenville, North Carolina, and Dyker Heights, Brooklyn, are famous for their elaborate Christmas light displays, which draw tourists from across the country.

317. Global Travel for Christmas Festivals: Christmas festivals like the Glastonbury Christmas Market in England or the German Christmas Market in Chicago attract global visitors eager to partake in European-style celebrations.

318. Christmas in Australia: Since Christmas occurs during the summer in the Southern Hemisphere, many

Australians celebrate with barbecues, beach picnics, and outdoor festivals instead of snow.

319. Christmas Travel Trends: More people are opting to travel early for Christmas (before December 20) to avoid the peak congestion, with many also extending their holidays into the New Year.

320. Christmas Road Trips: Driving for Christmas is a time-honoured tradition in many countries. Popular road trip routes include Route 66 in the U.S. and the Great Ocean Road in Australia, where travellers enjoy scenic winter landscapes.

321. Christmas in Japan: Although Christmas is not a public holiday in Japan, many tourists visit to experience its Christmas illuminations, shopping, and Western-inspired celebrations, particularly in cities like Tokyo.

322. Christmas in Lapland: Lapland in Finland is a magical Christmas destination. It is home to Santa Claus Village, where families travel to meet Santa and enjoy snowy adventures.

323. Christmas Travel and Safety: Holiday travel often involves increased traffic accidents, so emergency services see an uptick in demand. Safe travel tips, like checking weather conditions and road closures, become crucial.

324. Christmas at Disney Parks: Disneyland in California and Disney World in Florida are prime Christmas destinations, with elaborate decorations, themed parades, and festive performances drawing crowds from all over.

325. International Christmas Flights: Many people book international flights to visit family during the holidays, and countries like Mexico, India, and the Philippines are popular destinations for Christmas reunions.

326. Christmas in the Northern Lights: Places like Iceland, Norway, and Sweden attract travellers hoping to see the Northern Lights during the Christmas season, combining festive cheer with breathtaking natural phenomena.

327. Travel for Christmas Skiing: Christmas and New Year's are peak seasons for skiing holidays, with famous resorts seeing large crowds and long wait times but offering spectacular snowy experiences.

328. Christmas in the Amazon: Brazil and other parts of South America celebrate Christmas during the summer, with festivities like Parades, Christmas Eve Mass, and unique local traditions blending into a tropical Christmas atmosphere.

329. Christmas Shopping Abroad: Many people travel abroad for luxury Christmas shopping experiences.

Paris, London, and Milan are top choices for tourists seeking high-end brands and festive decorations.

330. Winter Solstice and Christmas Travel: Many cultures celebrate the winter solstice near Christmas. For example, in Peru, people travel to unique locations to mark this ancient celebration, which aligns with the Christmas season

Christmas Festivals and Events

331. Christkindlesmarkt, Nuremberg, Germany: One of the world's oldest and most famous Christmas markets, the Christkindlesmarkt dates to the 16th century and attracts millions of visitors annually.

332. Trafalgar Square Christmas Tree, London: A Christmas tree is donated yearly by Norway to the city of London in gratitude for British support during World War II. It is displayed in Trafalgar Square.

333. Reykjavik's Christmas Celebrations, Iceland: Reykjavik hosts festive events like the Yule Lads Parade and Christmas markets, along with the famous Christmas lights that cover the city.

334. The Christmas Lights at Dyker Heights, New York: Each year, the Dyker Heights neighbourhood in Brooklyn, New York, becomes a Christmas wonderland with extravagant light displays. Thousands of visitors come to see the area's famous holiday decorations.

335. Las Posadas, Mexico: A nine-day celebration leading up to Christmas Eve, Las Posadas is a reenactment of Mary and Joseph's search for a place to stay in Bethlehem, with participants going from house to house.

336. Cavalcade of Lights, Toronto, Canada: The Cavalcade of Lights is an annual event in Toronto, where the city's Christmas lights are switched on, accompanied by fireworks, performances, and a skating party.

337. Fête des Lumières, Lyon, France: Every December, Lyon holds the Fête des Lumières (Festival of Lights), where beautiful light displays and projections illuminate the city.

338. Santa Claus Village, Rovaniemi, Finland: In Rovaniemi, located in Finnish Lapland, visitors can meet Santa Claus and enjoy a variety of holiday-themed activities in the Santa Claus Village, which is open year-round but especially popular at Christmas.

339. Christmas in the Park, San Jose, California: Christmas in the Park is an annual event in San Jose, where downtown transforms into a holiday wonderland with hundreds of holiday displays, an ice rink, and festive lights.

340. Glastonbury Christmas Market, England: Known for its magical atmosphere, the Glastonbury Christmas Market features artisanal gifts, food stalls, and festive performances, attracting thousands every year.

341. Festival of Trees, Salt Lake City, Utah: A charity event in Salt Lake City, the Festival of Trees features beautifully decorated trees, wreaths, and gingerbread houses on display to raise funds for children's health services.

342. Bergen Christmas Festival, Norway: Bergen, Norway's second-largest city, hosts a month-long Christmas festival with traditional markets, cultural performances, and beautiful Christmas decorations.

343. Kwanzaa Celebrations: Kwanzaa is an African American cultural holiday from December 26 to January 1, with events focusing on unity, heritage, and community. It's celebrated with music, dancing, and family gatherings.

344. Winter Wonderland, Hyde Park, London: Hyde Park Winter Wonderland is an annual event that features ice skating, a circus, a Christmas market, rides, and food stalls, becoming one of the largest winter festivals in the UK.

345. Zürcher Weihnacht, Zurich, Switzerland: The Zürcher Weihnacht is a Christmas market in Zurich with over 150 stalls selling crafts, gifts, and delicious food, and the Main Station becomes home to a magical Christmas tree.

346. The Nutcracker Ballet, USA and Worldwide: The Nutcracker ballet, based on E.T.A. Hoffmann's story, is a beloved Christmas tradition performed by ballet companies worldwide, including the famous New York City Ballet.

347. Christmas Eve in Vatican City: Vatican City hosts one of the world's largest and most prestigious Masses, led by the Pope at St. Peter's Basilica. Thousands of pilgrims attend every year.

348. Berlin Christmas Markets, Germany: Berlin is home to many Christmas markets, with Gendarmenmarkt being one of the most popular, offering food, crafts, and festive performances.

349. Festa de Natal, Brazil: In Brazil, Christmas celebrations are full of fireworks, parades, and family feasts. The Festa de Natal in Gramado is especially famous for its incredible light displays.

350. Newport Winter Festival, Rhode Island: Newport Winter Festival is Rhode Island's largest winter festival, featuring ice sculpting, a light display, and winter activities, with events for all ages.

351. Christmas in the Shambles, York, England: The Shambles, a medieval street in York, turns into a winter wonderland with Christmas markets, food stalls, and festive cheer.

352. Stockholm Christmas Market, Sweden: The Gamla Stan area in Stockholm hosts one of the oldest Christmas markets in Sweden, with a rich history of selling traditional Swedish holiday items and foods.

353. Christmas Festival at the White House, USA: Every year, the White House is transformed into a Christmas wonderland, featuring elaborate decorations, themed trees, and seasonal displays open to the public for viewing.

354. Tivoli Gardens, Copenhagen, Denmark: Tivoli Gardens in Copenhagen has become a magical Christmas experience, with rides, markets, and festive performances. It's one of the oldest amusement parks in the world.

355. Nativity Festival, Salt Lake City, Utah: Salt Lake City's annual Nativity Festival features over 700 nativity scenes worldwide, with performances and cultural activities celebrating the Christmas story.

356. Rovaniemi Santa Claus Village, Finland: Rovaniemi, in Finnish Lapland, is considered the official hometown of Santa Claus. Visitors can enjoy Christmas events, visit Santa's office, and experience the Arctic Circle.

357. Christmas on the Bayou, Louisiana: In Louisiana, Christmas on the Bayou celebrates the holiday with a parade of decorated boats along the bayous, a unique Christmas event highlighting the state's water culture.

358. Advent Calendar Tradition, Germany: Many towns celebrate Advent with large public Advent calendars. Nuremberg features a giant calendar that opens doors every day leading up to Christmas.

359. Giant Lantern Festival, Philippines: Held in San Fernando, this event features the creation of giant, colourful lanterns that light up the town square, drawing thousands to enjoy the holiday decorations.

360. Copenhagen's Christmas Market at Nyhavn, Denmark: The Nyhavn Christmas Market in Copenhagen is known for its quaint charm, picturesque harbor setting, delicious Danish pastries, and various crafts for sale.

Christmas Craft

361. Handmade Ornaments: Many people create their own Christmas tree ornaments using felt, wood, clay, or even recycled items to give their trees a personal, unique touch.

362. Origami Christmas Decorations: Origami (Japanese paper folding) is a fun craft that can be used to make beautiful Christmas decorations like stars, angels, and trees from colourful paper.

363. Wreath Making: Christmas wreaths made from natural materials like pinecones, holly, and evergreen branches are popular for hanging on doors or mantels during the holiday season.

364. DIY Advent Calendars: Many people create their own Advent calendars by filling small boxes, bags, or envelopes with treats or notes to count down the days until Christmas.

365. Hand-Painted Christmas Cards: Crafting personalized, hand-painted Christmas cards is a popular tradition for sending warm wishes to family and friends.

366. Pinecone Crafts: Pinecones are a popular craft material for creating Christmas tree ornaments, wreaths, garlands, and candle holders.

367. Salt Dough Ornaments: Salt dough ornaments are an easy and inexpensive Christmas craft. They can be shaped into stars, angels, or any festive shape and painted or decorated with glitter.

368. Paper Snowflakes: Paper snowflakes are a classic Christmas craft that is easy to make by folding and cutting paper into intricate designs, perfect for decorating windows and walls.

369. Christmas Stockings: DIY Christmas stockings made from felt, fabric, or even knitted materials are a popular craft, often personalized with names or embroidered designs.

370. String Art Ornaments: String art involves wrapping colorful threads around nails on a wooden board to create holiday designs like Christmas trees, stars, and Santa faces.

371. Cinnamon Stick Decorations: Cinnamon sticks are often used in Christmas crafts for ornaments, wreaths, and garlands due to their pleasant aroma and rustic appearance.

372. Fabric Christmas Trees: These small trees made from fabric scraps can be sewn, glued, or stuffed with cotton and decorated with buttons, beads, and ribbons for a homemade touch.

373. DIY Christmas Village: Crafting your own Christmas village with small figurines, houses, and lights is a great way to bring a festive scene to life and create a cozy atmosphere.

374. Beaded Christmas Ornaments: Beading is a craft that can create stunning Christmas tree decorations. Beaded stars, snowflakes, and garlands are viral.

375. Knitted or Crocheted Christmas Gifts: Handmade scarves, mittens, hats, and blankets make perfect Christmas gifts, especially when crafted in festive colours and designs.

376. Holiday Soap Making: Making homemade Christmas soaps with festive scents like cinnamon, peppermint, or cranberry is a fun and fragrant way to create personalized gifts.

377. Pompom Decorations: Pom-poms made from yarn can be turned into Christmas tree ornaments or garlands or used as embellishments on stockings and wreaths.

378. Christmas Candle Holders: Crafting candle holders from mason jars, glass bottles, or even natural elements like twigs, pinecones, or cranberries creates a cozy and festive atmosphere.

379. Holiday Picture Frames: Making a personalized Christmas picture frame with craft materials like ribbon, glitter, and small ornaments can turn your favourite holiday photos into special keepsakes.

380. Felt Santa Ornaments: Felt is a perfect material for making Christmas ornaments like Santa faces, reindeer, or elves. They are easy to cut, sew, and embellish.

381. DIY Snow Globes: Creating homemade snow globes with jars, mini figurines, fake snow, and glitter is a fun and magical Christmas idea for kids and adults alike.

382. Sugar Scrubs: Making homemade Christmas sugar scrubs using ingredients like sugar, coconut oil, and essential oils is a great craft to create beauty gifts with festive scents.

383. Holiday Photo Garland: A creative way to display holiday memories is by turning family photos into a fun garland. Print and hang your photos along a ribbon with clothespins or frames.

384. Christmas Tree Centrepiece: Crafting a Christmas tree centrepiece from foam, wire, or even cardboard can be a great addition to your holiday dinner table, decorated with baubles and small lights.

385. DIY Christmas Cards with Stamps: Using rubber stamps or making your stamp designs can create beautiful and unique Christmas cards that carry a personal touch.

386. Handmade Christmas Crackers: Christmas crackers, traditionally pulled during the holiday dinner, can be handmade with paper rolls, small gifts, and festive ribbons.

387. Snowman Soup: A cute craft idea for gift-giving, snowman soup is a fun "recipe" gift, often consisting of a packet of hot chocolate mix, marshmallows, and candy canes in a jar or bag decorated with snowman imagery.

388. Christmas Tree Garland: A festive garland made from beads, buttons, or even popcorn and cranberries is a fun way to decorate your Christmas tree or mantle.

389. Decoupage Christmas Decorations: Decoupage is a technique where paper cutouts (such as vintage Christmas images or napkins) are glued onto surfaces like wood or glass to create beautiful Christmas decorations.

390. Upcycled Christmas Crafts: Many people repurpose old or unused items for Christmas crafts. For example, turning empty toilet paper rolls into reindeer antlers or creating an advent calendar from cereal boxes is a fun and eco-friendly activity.

Trivia Questions

Christmas Traditions and Customs Trivia

1.   What is the name of the traditional Christmas bread eaten in Italy?

Answer: Panettone

2.   What is the name of the traditional Christmas dessert served in the UK?

Answer: Christmas pudding

3.   What is the day after Christmas called in the UK and other countries?

Answer: Boxing Day

4.   In which country do people celebrate Christmas by eating KFC for dinner?

Answer: Japan

5.   What is the name of the Christmas gift-bringer in Italy?

Answer: La Befana

6.   What do children traditionally hang by the fireplace for Santa to fill with gifts?

Answer: Stockings

7.   What is the name of the Christmas Eve tradition where people hide a pickle ornament on the tree?

Answer: The Christmas Pickle

8.   In what country did the Christmas tradition of hanging stockings originate?

Answer: Netherlands

9. What famous Christmas figure is based on the legend of St. Nicholas?

10. Answer: Santa Claus

11. In which country do people celebrate Christmas by attending a "Julefrokost" (Christmas lunch)?

Answer: Denmark

Christmas Songs Trivia

12. Who recorded the famous Christmas song "Last Christmas"?

Answer: Wham!

13. What Christmas song was originally written for Thanksgiving?

Answer: Jingle Bells

14. Which Christmas carol was written by James Lord Pierpont in 1857?

Answer: Jingle Bells

15. What Christmas song includes the lyrics, "I just want you for my own"?

Answer: All I Want for Christmas Is You

16. In the song "Rudolph the Red-Nosed Reindeer," what was the name of Rudolph's girlfriend?

Answer: Clarice

17. Which Christmas song's lyrics begin with "Sleigh bells ring, are you listening"?

Answer: Winter Wonderland

18. Who sings the famous Christmas song "Do They Know It's Christmas?"

Answer: Band Aid

19. Which Christmas song begins with "You better watch out; you better not cry"?

Answer: Santa Claus Is Coming to Town

20. What is in the song "The Twelve Days of Christmas" on the fifth day?

Answer: Five golden rings

21. Who sang the Christmas hit "Wonderful Christmastime"?

Answer: Paul McCartney

Christmas History and Facts Trivia

22. What was the first year Christmas was celebrated as an official holiday in the United States?

Answer: 1870

23. Which U.S. president banned Christmas trees in the White House in 1851?

Answer: Franklin Pierce

24. In which century was the first recorded use of "Christmas"?

Answer: 11th century

25. When did the tradition of sending Christmas cards begin?

Answer: 1843

26. What is the most significant Christmas gift ever given?

Answer: The Statue of Liberty (given to the U.S. by France in 1886)

27. Which Christmas beverage was first created in the 17th century?

Answer: Eggnog

28. Who brought the first Christmas tree to the White House?

Answer: Franklin Pierce

29. Where did the tradition of the Yule log originate?

Answer: Scandinavia

30.   When did Christmas lights first become popular?

Answer: Late 19th century

31.   Who invented the modern Christmas card?

Answer: Sir Henry Cole

Christmas Symbols and Decorations Trivia

32. What Christmas decoration is made of evergreen branches and symbolizes eternal life?

Answer: Wreath

33. What plant is traditionally hung above doorways for couples to kiss under during Christmas?

Answer: Mistletoe

34. Which tree ornament represents the star that guided the wise men to the birth of Jesus?

Answer: Star

35. What Christmas decoration is used to symbolize the light of Christ?

Answer: Christmas lights

36. What animal is often associated with pulling Santa's sleigh?

Answer: Reindeer

37. Which tree is traditionally used as a Christmas tree?

Answer: Fir tree

38. What flower is commonly associated with Christmas and represents the blood of Christ?

Answer: Poinsettia

39. What is the traditional colour of the Christmas stockings?

Answer: Red

40. What candy is shaped like a shepherd's crook and is a typical Christmas treat?

Answer: Candy cane

41. What symbol, often used as a decoration, represents the birth of Jesus and is sometimes displayed on lawns?

Answer: Nativity scene

Christmas Around the World Trivia

42. What country is credited with the creation of the first Christmas tree?

Answer: Germany

43. In what country do people celebrate Christmas with a big feast on Christmas Eve, known as "Nochebuena"?

Answer: Spain

44. In which country is the tradition of celebrating Christmas with a "Jólabókaflóð," or Christmas Book Flood?

Answer: Iceland

45. What is the name of the Christmas celebration in Mexico, marked by the "Posada" procession?

Answer: Las Posadas

46. What country celebrates Christmas with a "KFC" dinner on Christmas Eve?

Answer: Japan

47. In which country do children celebrate Christmas by receiving gifts from "Père Noël"?

Answer: France

48. What is the name of the Christmas festival celebrated in Australia, often during summer?

Answer: Christmas Barbecue or Christmas BBQ

49. In which country do people celebrate Christmas by eating a traditional seafood feast on Christmas Eve?

Answer: Italy

50. What is the name of the holiday celebrated by the Dutch, and is it like Christmas?

Answer: Sinterklaas

51. In which country do people celebrate "Feliz Navidad" as their primary Christmas greeting?

Answer: Mexico

Christmas Food Trivia

52. What is traditionally hidden inside a Christmas pudding?

Answer: A coin

53. What type of pie is commonly eaten in the United States at Christmas?

Answer: Pumpkin pie

54. Which food is often left out for Santa on Christmas Eve?

Answer: Milk and cookies

55. What type of meat is traditionally served in the UK for Christmas dinner?

Answer: Roast turkey or goose

56. What Christmas treat is made with sugar, butter, and corn syrup and is often served in various colours and shapes?

Answer: Fudge

57. What fruit is commonly used in a Christmas cake or pudding?

Answer: Raisins or dried fruit

58. What vegetable is frequently served as a side dish for Christmas dinner?

Answer: Brussels sprouts

59. What is the traditional Christmas drink in the United States?

Answer: Eggnog

60. What is the name of the traditional Christmas bread in Germany, often filled with dried fruit and nuts?

Answer: Stollen

61. Which spice is often used in Christmas cookies and other holiday foods?

Answer: Cinnamon

Santa Claus Trivia

62. In what year was the first image of Santa Claus published as we know him today?

Answer: 1863 (in Harper's Weekly)

63. What company is responsible for popularizing the modern image of Santa Claus with its advertisements?

Answer: Coca-Cola

64. What is the name of Santa Claus's wife?

Answer: Mrs. Claus

65. How many reindeer does Santa have, including Rudolph?

Answer: Nine

66. What is the name of Santa's workshop located at the North Pole?

Answer: Santa's Workshop

67. In the poem The Night Before Christmas, what is the description of Santa's sleigh?

Answer: "A miniature sleigh and eight tiny reindeer."

68. What color are Santa Claus's boots traditionally?

Answer: Black

69. How old is Santa Claus usually said to be?

Answer: 1,750 years old (based on St. Nicholas's life)

70. What is the name of Santa's reindeer that starts with a "C"?

Answer: Comet or Cupid

71. What holiday beverage is associated with Santa's workshop?

Answer: Hot chocolate

Miscellaneous Christmas Trivia

72. What Christmas tradition originated in Germany and is celebrated by exchanging small gifts during Advent?

Answer: Advent calendar

73. Which Christmas carol was first sung in 1818 in Austria?

Answer: Silent Night

74. What Christmas-themed ballet premiered in 1892?

Answer: The Nutcracker

75. What famous Christmas decoration is made from edible gingerbread dough?

Answer: Gingerbread House

76. What famous Christmas figure lives at the North Pole?

Answer: Santa Claus

77. What year did the U.S. Postal Service issue the first Christmas stamp?

Answer: 1962

78. What is the name of the holiday song that was first recorded by Bing Crosby in 1942?

Answer: White Christmas

79. How long is the Christmas season in Western Christianity?

Answer: 12 days (from Christmas Day to Epiphany)

80. What is the main character's name in How the Grinch Stole Christmas?

Answer: The Grinch

81. What Christmas character was created by Dr. Seuss in 1957?

Answer: The Grinch

Christmas Movies Trivia

82. In Home Alone, where is Kevin's family going when they leave him behind?

Answer: Paris

83. What 1946 Christmas movie stars Jimmy Stewart as a man who learns the value of life?

Answer: It's a Wonderful Life

84. What is the fictional town's name where the movie The Nightmare Before Christmas takes place?

Answer: Halloween Town

85. In A Christmas Story, what is the name of the little boy who wants a Red Ryder BB gun for Christmas?

86. Answer: Ralphie

87. In Elf, what is Buddy the Elf's favourite syrup?

Answer: Maple syrup

88. Which actor played Ebenezer Scrooge in the 1984 film A Christmas Carol?

Answer: George C. Scott

89. What year did the movie Home Alone come out?

Answer: 1990

90. What is the Grinch's dog's name in The Grinch Who Stole Christmas?

Answer: Max

91. What is the name of the main character in The Polar Express?

Answer: The Boy (also referred to as "the conductor" in the movie)

92. Who plays the role of Santa Claus in the 1994 movie The Santa Claus?

Answer: Tim Allen

93. In Love Actually, what gift does Mark give to Juliet?

Answer: A series of photographs of her (to express his Love)

94. Which Christmas movie features a girl named Clara who dreams of a Nutcracker Prince?

Answer: The Nutcracker and the Four Realms (or The Nutcracker ballet adaptation)

95. What is the name of the department store in Miracle on 34th Street?

Answer: Macy's

96. In National Lampoon's Christmas Vacation, what is Clark Griswold's main goal for Christmas?

Answer: To have the best Christmas lights display on the block

97. In The Holiday, what city does Kate move to from London?

Answer: Los Angeles

98. In Frozen, what song is sung by Elsa while she builds her ice palace?

Answer: "Let It Go"

99. Which actor voiced the Grinch in the 2018 animated version of How the Grinch Stole Christmas?

Answer: Benedict Cumberbatch

100. In The Santa Clause 2, what is the name of the "Mrs. Claus" character?

Answer: Carol

101. What Christmas movie features a character named Scrooge McDuck?

Answer: Mickey's Christmas Carol

102. In Die Hard, what is the name of the building where the Christmas party occurs?

Answer: Nakatomi Plaza

Christmas Songs Trivia

103. Who recorded the famous Christmas song "Last Christmas"?

Answer: Wham!

104. What Christmas song was originally written for Thanksgiving?

Answer: Jingle Bells

105. Which Christmas carol was written by James Lord Pierpont in 1857?

Answer: Jingle Bells

106. What Christmas song includes the lyrics, "I just want you for my own"?

Answer: All I Want for Christmas Is You

107. In the song "Rudolph the Red-Nosed Reindeer," what was the name of Rudolph's girlfriend?

Answer: Clarice

108. Which Christmas song's lyrics begin with "Sleigh bells ring, are you listening"?

Answer: Winter Wonderland

109. Who sings the famous Christmas song "Do They Know It's Christmas?"

Answer: Band Aid

110. Which Christmas song begins with "You better watch out; you better not cry"?

Answer: Santa Claus Is Coming to Town

111. What is in the song "The Twelve Days of Christmas" on the fifth day?

Answer: Five golden rings

112. Who sang the Christmas hit "Wonderful Christmastime"?

Answer: Paul McCartney

113. Which Christmas song was first released by Bing Crosby in 1942?

Answer: White Christmas

114. What 1970s Christmas song includes the line, "So this is Christmas, and what have you done"?

Answer: Happy Xmas (War Is Over) by John Lennon

115. Who performed the Christmas hit "Do You Hear What I Hear?" in 1962?

Answer: Bing Crosby

116. What Christmas song includes the line, "Peace on earth, goodwill to men"?

Answer: "I Heard the Bells on Christmas Day."

117. Who released the famous Christmas song "Happy Christmas (War Is Over)" in 1971?

Answer: John Lennon and Yoko Ono

Which Christmas song did Mariah Carey release in 1994 that became a holiday hit?

Answer: All I Want for Christmas Is You

118. Which 1990s song by a popular boy band features the lyrics, "I'll be home for Christmas"?

*Answer: NSYNC

119. Which song did Bing Crosby make famous in 1942, becoming the best-selling single ever?

Answer: "White Christmas"

120. Who first recorded "Blue Christmas," a song later popularized by Elvis Presley?

Answer: Doye O'Dell

121. What Christmas song did the Jackson 5 record in 1970?

Answer: I Saw Mommy Kissing Santa Claus

Thank You for Reading

Thank you for exploring the fascinating world of Christmas with Christmas Facts Unwrapped!

I hope these festive facts brought joy, curiosity, and a sprinkle of holiday magic to your season.

If you enjoyed this book, I'd be thrilled if you could leave a review on Amazon. Your feedback helps other readers discover the joy of holiday trivia and inspires future creations.

Stay Connected

Follow me for more fascinating facts and upcoming books: Instagram @ellafactfinder

Stay tuned for more books by Ella Factfinder on my Amazon Author Page.

What's Next?

Keep an eye out for my next release in the Facts Series! From holidays to history, there's always something surprising to learn.